Away

Evelyn Kenrick

Presentation by *BookLeaf Publishing*

Web: www.bookleafpub.com

E-mail: info@bookleafpub.com

ISBN: 9789357614238

First edition 2022

To Roly, may you rest peacefully.

ACKNOWLEDGEMENT

Thank you to Jo, Hailey, Diane and Bill for excepting me into your household and life. Portscatho was an adventure that keeps me smiling throughout the year, I can't wait to return. Thank you to Robyn and Nelly, for supporting me through the stresses at school and keeping me smiling. Thank you to Jyoti for the hugs and the jokes at break time. Thank you to Dr Wells and Mr Keeble for inspiring me. Thank you to Moe for accepting me into your arms and brightening the family with your joy. Thank you to my father for his truth and kindness, holding my hand with whatever I do. Thank you William, the best brother ever. xx

PREFACE

Through our world of complexion and despair, it's hard to spend time breathing, resting or just relaxing. When you reach your teenage years, your mind is filled with all the horrors of the world, without any adult conscience to filter them or understand why they are there. We spend nights staring at the ceiling bubbling with anxiety or staying up late trying to distract ourselves from the daily calamities. Trying to fight your exam stresses whilst also comprehending the pain and suffering around the world, knowing that you can't do anything about it. It is a relief and also stings. Here is my hope in this darkness for all anxious teenagers, children and adults, people like me who struggled to sleep at night. Away, is a lullaby book for all ages. Compiled with sweet laments, childhood memories and love poems for all who need it.

Anon

Come sweet serenade of the silent,
where the sea twirls in a cylinder above and
below
and where the water carries you off.

Where the boat sings gracefully below
the chilling ripples of the heart that beat and beat
anon,
and the tide sways gracefully, left, right.

Left and right, away you sway. Left, right,
left and right, anon, anon, the tide goes on and
on.
sway left... sway right... sway left... sway right.

Sweet child of mine, left then right.
Anon anon.

Water Babies

I want to announce to you, that I've fallen in love
with the skies above,
and it's not a boast or cry but a song.
Who am I?
If not particles of my mother sun,
to shine a light in my world.
She sparkled, and light joined with their air
inside our lungs.
Forevermore.

And upon that silly earth,
Where all the walrus' will roam,
upon the mountains and the earth, I will travel.
And when mother goes away, and father comes
here to stay, I will sleep.
Cradled in his arms, for he will love and care for
me in the dark.

Whale Song

May your head sleep,
peacefully and deep.
No sharks in their shivers,
no birds of the rivers.

and away, away
soon gently you'll sway,
you'll glide along the sea,
like snow under ski.

and in icy fresh water
we'll play hours my daughter
with the fish of the ice
in our family paradise.

Gently roll next to me,
there is nowhere safer to be.
Than the gentle giants calming shore,
for you are the one I've been waiting for.

Nebulae

Let there be starlight
for all who need it.
May it fall upon their heads tonight
and light their way out of any pit.

Let there be starlight
where all lights have faded
every morning, midday and night
let their lives big and small be saved.

Let their be spring in their winters,
hope in their frights,
hugs before bed,
and kisses goodnight.

Let there be starlight,
for the cold and unfound,
let there be starlight,
and no other sound.

My Sun

I tucked him up tight,
and kissed him once more.
The little boy yawned
"Please stay a bit more?"

But the birds were nesting,
the twigs cuddled them.
And the fish were sleeping,
the river pillowed them.
Sharks were not shivering,
the sea warmed their hearts.
And people were snoring,
the drink hit them hard.

The sky was asleep
it had closed its eyes.
It only saw black,
Only heard goodnights.
But the boy was not-
asleep like the rest.
It wanted to play,
in the blanket space.

Round his glowing head,
the planets all swayed,

The stars in the night
so still they stayed.
To help the little boy,
close his eyes tight
Three, two, one.
Little boy, goodnight.

Bird Watchers

I may tease my grandmother,
for hastily grabbing her special binoculars
to see the buzzard flying over the hedge.
Or tease my grandfather,
for rummaging for his immaculate camera
to take the greatest photo of said creature.
Even though we both know,
it'll be a blurred photo of his eyebrows.
And I don't deny I tease them,
for loving something I take for granted.
But I do appreciate the bird.

With its delicate feathers connected to its hull.
Its wings that swim afloat in the wind.
It's beak and shiny eyes like mirrors of the night.
I do appreciate the bird. I always have.
For like us it has a family.

A home made of sticks instead of bricks.
A father, mother, a sister, and a brother.
A wife to love, a family to cuddle.
And that's all I know to be true.
All things are connected by love.
It does not matter how it came to be,
all that matters is that it loves.
That's true beauty to me.

Puddle

Stars are not shown for those who require the
light to see,
they are hidden and quiet as the invisible breeze.
Yet with stars you see exactly what you to
expect,
some spheres of light that seem to connect.

Small oceans, showing you what you already
see.
And they never show you what you want.
Your face staring back in disappointment,
that now your shoes are wet.

Shooting Stars

Trapped in cages of gloom and despair,
But hope will abound. For the stars are
shining through the creaks and cracks.
The stars that are seen by love and
dears across the moon kissed earth.
So, while I"m alone I know I'm free.
From the grief of leaving them alone.
Their eyes sparkling with glee.
As even though they'll forget me,
they'll remember me somewhere.
Memories fluttering like butterflies.
I'll stay trapped happily forevermore.
For we had the best of times.

Agrypnia

Don't fall asleep, don't sink too deep,
into an endless ocean of rest.
Keep talking to me, then maybe I'll be,
still awake for us to talk even more.

It's way too late, I should got to sleep.
I've got stuff to do in the sunrise.
But time with you isn't too wasted hastily,
and I don't want to go away.

Keep me close in your arms.
The real world can wait a bit longer.
I don't want to sleep, because I don't want to go
away from you into a land of slumber.

Dreaming isn't quite the same
as talking and watching the stars
in your eyes, I don't need sleep.
I don't want to go away.

Sinking away, for the new day
that comes closer from a mile to an inch.
I know you'll go but tomorrow.
I'll still be right by your side.

Now fall asleep, nice and deep,
into an endless ocean of rest.
Close up those lips, hush little prince,
I see you in the morning for us to talk some
more.

Everest

The feeling where your legs are cobbles and
pebbles
that shake and scrape to drag you down.
Where the strings of your heart are tied to your
feet
and the world keeps spinning round and round.

Where the snow crinkles like salt and vinegar
crips,
and the taste in your mouth is coarse and sour,
upon the fort you don't dare to move.
And each breath feels as dense as bread without
flour.

You stop at the next bench, with pillows as
cushions.
And you fall down sideways in a pile on your
breast,
they day has been long and there will be many
more.
But for now, more than ever - rest.

Icegloom

I'm at the pond again,
it's frozen over in the winter chill.
White and blue shapes
form a smooth cress.

I make a house for the hedgehogs
out of cubes and snow as the bricks
mixed with some crushed ice as the cement
even though it freezes my fingers.
Bit by but I layer up my circle,
like the igloo, but pale grey.
as the pond stains the snow
to different colours of mouldy steel.
Layer by layer I climb up,
and I place sticks to hold it up.
Imaging the badgers watching by
who want to use the igloo.

But then the sun rises,
all the bruises are healed.
The house is left alone.
In the morning it melts,
but the squirrels found a new home.

Melorism

Begin and end, dawn and the dusk,
the light and the dark, metal and rust.
Time falling away, dust and the sand.
Beauty and mortal go hand in hand.

Birds dip their toes in ponds of glass,
and at the time the fish will start to dance.
Cobwebs and mist when time is right,
create diamonds in moonlight.

Fish scales colour the water gleam,
rainbow cascades of deep purple and green.
the sun rises upon the blue,
all of life begins to sing their tune.

Truth and hope, love and lust,
the light and the dark, metal and rust.
Creation knit and let life grow,
words don't need sense for love to show.

Sundays

Roast pork with crackling in a prickling blaze,
fat cheeks and greasy forks about,
the smiley mouths in focus with one another,
"Darling can you pass me another Guinness
please?"

A lazy rainy day you say, a family day for us.
Where we sloth in peace on splendid sofas
no smiles, but yawns in ignorant bliss
at this strange world of working wonder.

Unbeneath the small yellow lights and amber
aura of the lounge. We don't mutter
just watch the car show with the safe fire
the smell of mint toothpaste and dark chocolate.
The Sunday smiles I wish I saw all week
sketched on our faces.

Our weekend wear, our holiday hearts.
Maybe the world would be kinder?
If we desired peace over money,
and beer rather than champagne,
hugs rather than depressed fossils,
slowly getting younger.

Dolphins

Like dancing stars we play unchallenged,
eternal light drifting through each dust
and each dust cries out in song.
"Help I'm dying the net is pulling me in!"

The fish are made of stardust
and the nets are blessed of time.
Grandfather always says that hope is on its way.
And so the net crawls through the sea.

Time is running out,
I'm running out of breath.
Time is running out,
but the sea dogs hear my cry.

The dolphins grab my hand
and lead me towards the light.
Where the old men come to die.
But we are all made of stardust
and a reborn in the stars,
when the sun comes up.

Hibernate

Let the trickle of spring in the sunny sky
where my lover dances the hours and darkness
goodbye,
shine stars of fluorescent moonlight onto their
breast.
And in warm skipping grass and rose they lay to
rest.
To awake only when one human loves another
equally,
and peace in our time will bring us together.

By Heart

I know the way to home, beneath the sun.
It lies on groves of leafy sticks untouched
by the cruel hands of dark winter and frost.
Where the deepest of poisoned souls alit
with violence, craft our horrid world.

Where is the world I was promised in time?
Why are all the trees smoked in fumes now.
Why can't I see the stars tonight? Father,
where did they all go behind the dark storm.
Can I go home yet? I know the way there.

You follow the lonely pebbled path,
and look for where concrete turns to grass.
There be the treasure.
A world as fragile as glass.

Malvern Hills

There is a knight within the mist,
his shiny metal clinks in the gust
echoing in passing.
He walks like a ship through the sea,
plowing through the cloud. And
he looks for his kin.
Another knight in the dark of
a cave, wings scarred by trauma
and battle in vain.
The knight of black in his cave.
There is a silver knight on a green hill
who searches for his kin until
the sun closes in.

Maybe one day the knight will find
his brother of darkness in the ground
before the sun closes in.
And nightmares start to dance.

There we watch the sunfall,
the knights will wait for another new dawn.

King George

George danced and jumped down the trail
towards the sandy beach,
with one welly on foot and a bottle of juice in
his hand
he skipped towards the sea.

Behind the young lad ran his brother
with hot chocolate in his grasp.
He did not have a welly, nor sandals of sorts,
just bare toes in the grit.

They banged sticks against poles,
dug holes in the ground,
and build castles of sand and stone.

They placed flags in the world,
swords in the earth
and their drinks they gulped with a laugh.

The two little brothers roamed this country.
Until at sunset they reached home.

Rift

The sand drips in its hourglass as it flows
between the wetsuit socks of my left and right
feet.
It crinkles, in shivering ripples as I shudder in
the harsh breeze.
I drag my float wrapped around my waist to the
brink of the ocean blue, as the seaweed dance in
the waves. I quake in the frigid water.
There is a fine line between insanity and genius.

I thrust my board into the sea, it clashes with
rolling water and foam creeps over the edges as
a ghost.
I jump on, my ankle attached to the strap which
scratches my skin, but nonetheless I continue to
glide along the shore water. I grip my paddle and
race to calmer tides.

Then I balance my paddle on the front of the
board. The waves gush around me. But with the
glassy water sounds and the deep blue beneath
the rainy waters I close my eyes and hold my
breath. Slowly lifting my knees to balance.

Afloat I stand, delicately perched on the blue on
the blue.
Until the tide takes me back.

Shoreline

How can the horizon be so still, it weaves and
holds the sun in a basket.
Waves are small unimportant ripples that cannot
disturb
the perpendicular gaze to the clouds. As the
waves
trickle against the stones, now shining with salty
gleam.
But rain is mixing with the gloomy murk of the
shore-water
and now the mixture is filling with sand.

Is there much better than a storm shrouded
shoreline>
Nature and Fortune has blessed me with a
paradise
at the shore. With an open window to see the
sea.
Not that there was much to see now, the sun was
slowly
dipping its legs shyly into the darkness.

Home may not be in my head,
my house is in the fields,
but my heart is on the shoreline of Portscatho.

Elegy to Roly

Your smiles rebounded sunlight,
your body was a jumping joy,
you played and ran into the night.
You were the most handsome boy.

I did not see you very long,
but my heart will be yours to bear.
You chased all the days away headstrong;
your excitement everywhere.

But now it's time to roll away,
towards the soil and flowerbed deep.
To find fresh clouds up there to play
wrapped in blissful, eternal sleep.